I HOPE YOU DIE SOON

I HOPE YOU DIE SOON

Words on Non-Duality and Liberation

Richard Sylvester

NON-DUALITY PRESS

For Jo and Sam

And in deep gratitude to Jen, Tony and Claire.
Without you this book would not have been written.

Published by Non-Duality Press

6 Folkestone Rd, Salisbury SP2 8JP
United Kingdom
www.non-dualitybooks.com

First printing March 2006
Copyright © Richard Sylvester 2005
Copyright ©Non-Duality Press 2005
Cover design John Gustard

ISBN 978-0-9551762-1-0

It is not easy to write a book about nothing.

Contents

Introduction

The most common misconception about liberation is that it is something an individual can gain. But liberation is a loss—the loss of the sense that there ever was a separate individual who could choose to do something to bring about liberation.

When it is seen that there is no separation, the sense of vulnerability and fear that attaches to the individual falls away and what is left is the wonder of life just happening. Instead of meaning there is a squirrel motionless on a grey tree trunk, legs splayed, head up, looking straight at you. Instead of purpose there is the astonishing texture of cat's fur or the incredible way an ant crawls over a twig. The loss of hope is no loss when it is replaced by the moorhens bobbing on the lake.

When the sensation that I am in control of my life and must make it happen ends, then life is simply lived and relaxation takes place. There is a sense of ease with whatever is the case and an end to grasping for what might be.

ON LIBERATION

Preliminaries

Liberation cannot be described in words. It cannot be understood by the mind. It cannot be seen until it reveals itself. Then no words or ideas are able to express it and no mind is able to grasp it.

Yet liberation is all there is. Right now.

Paradox.

The seeing of liberation has nothing to do with the mind. Yet here liberation is, covered over by the mind. Covered over by the mind which does not exist.

Paradox.

Liberation is the end of searching and the end of meaning. Liberation reveals the meaning of life as life itself. There can be no searching for that which is seen already to be the case.

Language by its nature describes duality—events, experiences, things, thoughts, feelings. Phenomena. The stuff that happens. There is no language to describe non-duality. The best we can do is to hint at it.

So let us hint.

Awakening:
Seeing there is No One

It begins with Saturday afternoons in Hampstead, listening to discussions about non-duality held by Tony Parsons. I do not understand a lot of what is said but something keeps drawing me there. And I like the jokes and the conversation and the drinking afterwards so I go back again and again.

Then at a central London station on a warm summer evening the person, the sense of self, suddenly completely disappears. Everything remains as it is—people, trains, platforms, other objects—yet everything is seen for the first time without a person mediating or interpreting it. There are no flashing lights, no fireworks, none of the whirligig phenomena of LSD or hallucinogenic mushrooms. But this is the real 'wow', seeing an ordinary railway station for the first time without any sense of self. Here is the ordinary seen as the extraordinary, arising in oneness with no one experiencing it.

In that instant it is seen that there is no one. The sense of there being a person has been a constant up to this point and given meaning to this life. For so many years it has never been questioned. It has been so thoroughly taken for granted as me, my centre and location, that it has not even been noticed. Now it is seen as a complete redundancy. Suddenly it is known that I never had a life because there never was an 'I'. In a split second of eternity it is known that without an 'I' everything is being seen for the first time simply as it is. I do not live, I am lived. I do not act, but actions happen through me, the divine puppet.

Every concern of this small but so important apparent life falls away in an instant.

Within a second, the self returns saying "What the hell was that?" But that split-second of no one brings about irrevocable changes to the internal landscape. For seeing this can blow your mind.

The past becomes two-dimensional. Before this, the past was a three dimensional landscape which I visited frequently. I rushed about in it, jumping from place to place; every scene had energy and reality to it. That energy appeared as feelings and thoughts, mostly about regret and guilt, with themes of "What if…" and "If only…" endlessly playing. The past was consequently tilled and re-tilled, different possibilities uselessly played out as if obsessive revisiting could somehow change the geography, bring back a lost lover or erase some offence given or received. Now, after that split second of no one, although the person has come back, the past is like a flat painting. All the scenes are still there—this is not Alzheimer's—but they have no energy, no reality, and there is little impulse to visit any of them anymore. Occasionally one scene or another from the past flickers into life for a while but then it dies away again. Regret and guilt loosen their grip.

Issues and problems still arise but they cannot hang around for as long as they used to do. The rock face which gave toe holds for them to clamber up and grab me by the throat is starting to crumble. The internal landscape has become slippery. As Nisargadatta says, the world is full of hoops, the hooks are all ours. Now the hooks are dissolving. However, during the next year the self frantically tries to reassert itself, sometimes apparently very successfully as issues manage to re-emerge, as boredom, despair, emotional pain somehow still have to be experienced.

One thing that is immediately seen is the nature of all the apparent spiritual experiences that arose during the years of searching and following false paths and gurus. Suddenly they are seen for what they really are, emotional and psychological experiences happening to an unreal person and no more significant than putting on a shoe or having a cup of coffee.

Spiritual experiences are not difficult to evoke. Meditate intensively, chant for long periods, take certain drugs, go without food or sleep, put yourself in extreme situations. That will probably do it. I had done all of these things and there had been many spiritual experiences. I had chanted for hours and meditated to the beating of mighty Tibetan gongs. I had seen the guru, sitting on a dais in impressive robes, dissolve into golden light before my eyes. Personal identity had refined and dissolved in transcendental bliss. The universe had breathed me as my awareness expanded to fill everything.

So what?

There had always been someone there, having the spiritual experience. A person, no matter how refined, had always been present. These events had all happened to 'me'. None of them had anything more or less to do with liberation than stroking a cat.

And anyway "You can't stay in God's world for very long. There are no restaurants or toilets there."

Liberation is not personal and has nothing to do with any psychological, emotional or 'spiritual' experience, no matter how refined it may be. A spiritual or psychological experience is just a personal experience. Once it is seen that I am nothing, it is also seen that any experience arises only for an *apparent* person and falls away again in oneness with no significance at all. There is no real person in whom the experience arises and no possibility that it could have any meaning.

And liberation has nothing to do with the absence or presence of problems or issues, which may or may not continue to arise.

Liberation does not bring unending bliss. For that, try heroin, prozac or a lobotomy.

What a relief. Liberation does not require you to be any particular way.

Liberation does not require 'you' to be at all. A person is not writing these words. Oneness is writing these words. And oneness is reading them.

Within the story, the period of awakening lasts for one year. During this time, the person reasserts itself, sometimes strongly, drops away again and returns. For a while there is a desert where personal pain is as intense as before but all the old comforts and mechanisms for dealing with it have lost their meaning. A particular comfort had been the belief that pain was meaningful, necessary to my spiritual evolution. "There's no gain without pain." Now that thought simply appears ridiculous. I am beginning to understand that this awakening is ruthless, stripping away every belief that I have ever held and ever clung to. Now there are no life rafts left, not even a piece of driftwood.

It is sometimes said that this ruins your life. Well, it ruins what you thought was your life. And there is a saying I remember at this point. "Why do you want liberation? How do you know you'd like it?"

My God. Things have got worse, not better. For previously there was hope.

Liberation:
Seeing 'I' am Everything

Within the story, a year after awakening, I am standing in a shop in an ordinary country town. Suddenly but with great gentleness the ordinary is displaced by the extraordinary. The person again disappears completely and now it is seen clearly that awareness is everywhere and everything. The localised sense of self is revealed to be just an appearance. There is no location, no here or there. There is only oneness appearing as everything and this is what 'I' really am. 'I' am the shop, the people, the counter, the walls and the space in which everything appears. When the self disappears, and awareness is seen as everything, then this is seen for what it is, a wonderful hologram sustained by love.

At a certain time as a child, awareness appears to coagulate into a discrete space, becoming solid and separate from everything else. This is what creates the sense of 'me' with its hopes and fears and loves and burdensome responsibilities. The thoughts and feelings and sensory phenomena, which really simply arise in awareness, are now owned by someone, are now felt to belong to 'me'. And so the drama of being a person starts.

There is no locality to awareness other than 'everywhere'. There is only liberation. But in liberation the sense that 'I' am not liberated can and does arise. It manifests as the sense of separation, of being located over here rather than over there, separate from all other people and things. It brings fear, longing and hope, and it is highly addictive. It cannot see through itself and it may simply continue for seventy or eighty years until it ends at death. Or it may end sooner, anywhere, at any time.

Liberation is freedom from the burden of being a person who apparently has to make choices and decisions; choices and decisions which have consequences. What a wonderful relief it is to see that there is no choice, no person, no separation. Nothing you have ever done has ever led to anything because you have never done anything. No one has ever done anything although it appears that things have been done.

Isn't it wonderful that you have never made a choice in your life? There is nothing to regret, nothing to feel guilty about. Nothing could ever have been any different, nothing could ever have been any other way. Isn't that a relief? Nothing matters. There is nowhere to go. There is nothing that has to be done. There is no meaning and no morality. There is no help and no hope. You can let it all go, you can release all the tension. You can begin to enjoy the wonder of hopelessness and the gift of meaninglessness. You can begin to enjoy your complete helplessness.

In liberation it is seen that nothing has any meaning, it is simply what it is. The story does not stop. The story continues but now it is seen that it is just a story. All the passions of your apparent life are *just stuff happening.* The conflicts, the loves, the struggles for control and power, the victories and defeats are simply phenomena arising in oneness and falling away again with no meaning at all.

Nothing has any more significance than anything else or could ever be greater or lesser. The Trojan war and a glass of beer are equal.

Except, of course, to the mind.

You cannot earn liberation. I have not earned liberation. No one will ever earn liberation. You cannot become good enough or work hard enough or be sincere enough to deserve it. Liberation has not happened to me and it will not happen to you. Yet there is liberation. There is only ever liberation. Perfection is already here. What you are is already divine.

Searching will not get you anywhere, but there is nothing wrong with searching. In this apparent process it may be heard that searching is meaningless but searching cannot be given up until it stops. Then it is over and it is seen that what you were searching for has always been with you, in fact it has always been what you are. But to suggest that you give up searching in order to find is pointless. It does not matter whether you get drunk, meditate, read the paper, sit with the guru or go to the races. None of these will make liberation any more or any less likely. Searching or not searching, meditating or not meditating, misses the point. For there is no one who can choose to do any of these things. If meditation happens, it happens and it will go on happening until it does not. It is the same for getting drunk. You may as well give up the belief that you can choose anything.

Except that you cannot do that either.

Until it happens.

Liberation is what is left when the self is gone.

But the self is simply liberation arising as the self.

Liberation is what is happening while you search for liberation.

Inside, you already know this.

Being Awake and Being Asleep are the Same—unless You are Asleep

When liberation is seen, it is known that being awake in liberation is no different from being asleep. They are both seen simply as oneness, manifesting as sleep or awakeness. In liberation all the mystification of enlightenment is stripped away and its absolute ordinariness is revealed. Mountains are seen simply as mountains.

But to the seeker who is still asleep, and in their sleep is searching restlessly for an end to the sense of separation, there appears to be a chasm between that state and liberation. Liberation seems like a marvellous prize to be attained, promising blissful feelings, freedom from pain and suffering, an end to all problems, perhaps magical powers and of course the jealous admiration of your friends. This is why the search for liberation can be so desperate and the question "Will I get it?" so powerful.

All that prevents the seeing of liberation is the thought "I am not liberated". So some say that what you must do to see liberation is to drop this thought. But there is no one who can choose to do this. The thought that this is not liberation, which is the same as the thought "I am separate" or "I am searching", continues until it drops away. The apparent self can do nothing to discover that it is itself an illusion—an appearance cannot discover reality.

Liberation is seen either while the body-mind is still functioning or at the death of the body-mind and it does not matter which, except in the story. "At death there is only liberation. It is just more chic to see liberation when you are alive."

In liberation it is seen that there never was anything to seek. What you seek has always been with you, what you are has always been what you are. When this is seen all searching ends.

I Hope You Die Soon

Once upon a time I was a busy seeker, meditating sincerely, being careful with my karma, receiving shaktipat, having my chakras opened and cleansed by blessed gurus, thinking I was going somewhere.

Then catastrophe struck. I met Tony Parsons. And that was the end of what I thought had been my life. Tony, who hugged me at the end of one of his meetings and said to me "I hope you die soon." Tony, to whom I feel the most profound gratitude, even though there is no one.

There is no more appropriate way to end this. Let me simply pass on the blessing I was given and say to you "I hope you die soon."

THE STUFF THAT
HAPPENS

Language

A word is not the phenomenon it names. A description of the scent of mown grass is not the scent of mown grass. Words can only point to liberation and even then only in a misleading way. A description of liberation, which in any case is an impossibility, could not convey the scent of liberation.

Words can only describe phenomena. Liberation is neither a phenomenon nor a collection of phenomena.

Nevertheless if there is to be a discourse about anything, including liberation, it can only be carried on in words.

But there is also silence. Just as here the black print only makes sense because it appears against a white background.

All language is suspect. But in this book the following words should be regarded with especial suspicion and always be read as if in quotation marks because the assumption contained in each of them is false:

mind   person   past   future   now

then	time	place	here	there
I	you	me	choice	freedom

The word 'I' in the sentence "I am happy" has exactly the same force as the word 'It' in the sentence "It is raining." There is no 'it'. There is no 'I'. Rain simply falls. Happiness simply arises.

Most writing that purports to be about non-duality is absolutely dualistic. As soon as a writer suggests that there is someone who can do something to bring about liberation, you are reading nonsense. Often it will be highly articulate, fluent, complex and persuasive nonsense.

The Mind

If liberation is seen, it is seen. If not, not. That's just the way it is.

In the Upanishads it is said "Advaita is not an idea. *It is!* The lightning flashes, the eye blinks... Then? You have either understood or you have not understood... If you have not understood, too bad!"

Tough, isn't it.

It seems so unfair to the mind that nothing can be done.

The mind can confuse and the mind can clarify. Most of the time there is confusion. Occasionally there is clarity. The mind chatters incessantly, insisting that its nonsense makes sense.

The mind is like a loop tape which plays all day long with just one message recorded on it. "See, I'm right. See, I'm right." It comes complete with a device which filters out all evidence to the contrary.

The mind insists that it can bring us to personal enlightenment. And yet it has to recognise that enlightenment has still not happened. The mind can never deliver on its promise, so it says that we have not meditated enough or chanted enough mantras or shown enough devotion to the guru. Or we have not been sincere enough or done enough work on clearing our chakras or performed enough purifying rituals. Or we have not searched hard enough to find the final secret. Or of course that we have searched too hard.

The mind believes in justice, in fairness. The mind believes that virtue and effort should be rewarded. If only I would try harder to become a more spiritual person, bliss would be mine. The mind thinks that liberation must bring a state of permanent bliss because it sees liberation as a reward for hard work done, the result of grace that has been earned.

And so the tread mill of beliefs and evolutionary paths continues and gurus flourish.

When it is first seen that there is no one, the mind may be left shattered. But usually it rapidly reassumes control. The mind can only see awakening as a personal experience. Surely, the mind says, there must be a way that I can recreate this wonderful happening, hold on to it for longer, suck out its marrow, finally live in it for ever.

The mind's failure to do any of this may lead to despair.

When there is a sudden awakening, the complete disappearance of the person for a split second, all the concerns that have dogged that particular life immediately fall away because suddenly there is no one to feel concern. In an instant the mind is blown and all the contracted energy bound up with the 'past' and the 'future' is released. It is seen that there is absolutely no possibility of personal suffering or of anything mattering because now the person is seen not to exist. Depression? Anxiety about a job interview? Hope that Louise loves me? Fear about my medical test results next week? Suddenly in emptiness there is no one who owns any of this.

But a split second later it is probable that the self will return with all its self-concerns.

For this character, during the period of awakening, the absolute fragility of the appearance is seen. Streets, people, buildings, fields, hills are all seen to have neither substance nor duration. Everything is simply a play of colour, a film of light hanging in nothing and lasting not even for a moment. A moment has duration with a beginning, a middle and an end, and the appearance has none of these. Everything appears two dimensionally like a picture postcard. There is no embodiment from which voices on the telephone appear—it is unsettling to realise that my friends' voices, as they phone me, are entirely disembodied.

Spiritual Experiences

Spiritual experiences are simply a form of personal psychological, emotional and physical experience. In even the most refined forms of transcendence there is always someone there having the experience. However, this cannot be known until it is seen even for a split second that there is no one.

Spiritual experiences can be evoked by personal effort just as a wall can be painted by personal effort. But they cannot be sustained for long just as no experience can be sustained for long.

The mind loves putting effort into creating spiritual experiences and enjoys the rewards they bring. To the mind it seems so just. I put in a certain amount of effort and I get out a certain reward.

It is just the same when baking apple pies.

The mind says that when enough spiritual effort has been made enlightenment will be mine, perhaps in another ten lifetimes. But once it is seen that there is no one, it is seen that I have never made any effort, I have never done any work and nothing is given to me as a reward. No part of my life can possibly have anything to do with me.

In a split second of awakening all the comforts of the spiritual path can disappear. All the efforts made, the fun and busyness of packing to go to India, the ashrams arduously visited, the meaningful travelling around the spiritual bazaar, the kundalini awakenings and the shaktipats received may be seen to have led nowhere and to have counted for nothing.

Seeing this can produce ripples of laughter or a desert of despair. For when I come back after awakening, I may have got the joke or I may truly feel alone and without hope.

This may lead to a period of just sitting. In laughter or despair.

Being a Person

The sense of a being a person is so strong. It has been with me all my life and it is the strongest addiction of all. It arises in so many ways.

I have responsibilities. I am a father to two children. I have students. I am chairman of this very important committee. Perhaps I can save the planet in my spare time.

I have fears. Perhaps I have cancer. My house might have dry rot. I might end my days lonely in a single room with dribble down my chin. Maybe on my way to my holiday destination the aeroplane will come screaming out of the sky in flames.

I have hopes. Perhaps I will meet someone in the coffee bar today and fall in love. Maybe I will be promoted at work. I might win the lottery and be able to give up work and buy a Ferrari at last.

I have longings. Many of these are contradictory. I yearn for inclusion and for solitude, for independence and to be looked after, to feel deeply and to be impregnable and unmoved.

I live in a state of contraction, tensed against threat and pain. There is an overwhelming sense that I am in here and everything else is out there bearing down on me. I have to protect myself against all the pressures that could destroy me. I even have to protect myself against my own dear ones, perhaps especially against those who have seen me at my most open. I may be pulled in every direction by contradictory impulses. Because of my yearning for unity I want to be close to another, to be intimate, to be held, to be comforted. Because of my fear of being invaded, I want to be separate, to be distant, to be autonomous. No state can ever bring me satisfaction for long because every state that I desire contradicts a different state that I also want. When I am included I crave separation. When I am excluded I crave belonging.

I am vulnerable, separate, fearful, easily put out, easily put down. I travel between ecstasy and despair, or I remain imprisoned in armoured non-feeling. Above all I have memories of the past and fears and fantasies about the future. I have regrets, guilt, wishes, if onlys, self-consciousness, embarrassment. I am charismatic or shy. I play my games, exercise my ego, know that I am right, justify myself, evangelise for my beliefs. The sense of 'I' is constantly being created and recreated by every phenomenon, every thought, sensation and feeling.

It is unimaginable that life can go on without the sense of me, that this can simply be seen with no one seeing it. It is impossible to imagine the seeing that there is no one, for who would be seeing it?

Since the first moment of separation the person has been ever-present. Then suddenly in a split second the sense of 'I' drops away completely. There is no gradual transcendental diffusion of the person but its complete disappearance. And the unimaginable has happened, the total absence of self has been seen. The void has been recognised. All concepts of space and time become meaningless. There is only omnipresence. Here and there are seen to be the same.

After this it is very difficult to take your previous life seriously.

The Great Mantra

There is no method, but if there were it might be to repeat the mantra 'hopeless, helpless and meaningless'. It would be good, during this repetition, to notice that there is no one doing it. But there is no one who can notice this either.

The person believes there is hope and goes out to seek for that hope to be fulfilled. At the root of this seeking is the thought "This isn't it but if I can change it sufficiently it might become it." But hope is always disappointed eventually when it is realised that this lover isn't it either, this car isn't it, this Tuscan villa isn't it, this guru isn't it. Hope leads to disappointment and then either to despair or to another futile hope. Hope can never lead you from "This isn't it" to "This is it" because all the time that you are thinking "This isn't it", really it is. You can't get from where you are to 'it' because you are already here.

If only it were possible to give up hope. Yet hope may fall away and this can be a great blessing.

The person believes there is help. But you cannot be helped to become what you already are. It is as if you are sitting in a handsome chair and saying "Please tell me how I can get to sit in that chair. That chair over there so far away from me. It looks so beautiful. I know my life will work if I can only get to sit in that chair." What can be said? "But you are already sitting in it, where is there to go?" You cannot hear this if you believe yourself to be somewhere else. So what can be said when you ask "Help me to become liberated"? There is already only liberation. No one can help you attain that which is already the case. That is why in Zen it is sometimes said "I'd love to give you something helpful but we don't have anything."

You are alone in your complete helplessness. There is nothing you can either do or avoid doing. If that could be known, then striving might come to an end and in that relaxation liberation might be seen. But that begins to sound like a method and there is no method for there is no one who can give up striving.

The person believes there is meaning. But it is a priceless gift to see that everything is meaningless. Everything that apparently arises is just stuff happening. It has no implications and it is going nowhere. When it is seen that nothing has any meaning there can be such relief. Every tension in your apparent life might fall away. But the mind hates this. The mind cries out "The Holocaust? Salvation through the blood of the lamb? The enlightenment of Buddha under the bodhi tree?

The shamanic signs that I will find my soul-mate? Dead Aunt Maud's spirit telling me 'The lost key to the back door is in the tea urn.' Surely such events must have significance."

Yet none of this is going anywhere. Nothing is leading to anything. The Holocaust and redemption through faith and Buddha and shamanic signs and dead Aunt Maud are simply thoughts arising and distracting you from seeing this. Oneness is distracting itself from noticing that it is not two. That is the game. Every thought of separation, each thought that does not notice that there is only unconditional love, simply keeps the game going.

If there were any point in telling you to give up hope and meaning and see your utter helplessness, I would. But there is no one to tell you this and no one to listen.

You can neither search nor give up searching. Searching will happen of its own accord until it stops. If you try to give up searching, you will search for a method to give up searching.

The Impeccable Behaviour of the Enlightened Ones

There is only liberation. Typing these words is liberation. Reading them is liberation. Drinking tea is liberation. The self is liberation manifesting as the self. But while the self, the apparent person, is there, it prevents liberation being seen. It cannot know liberation because it is looking for it. As long as it is believed that this is not it, there is tension and separation. It is felt that the self is not good enough, that it always has to do something more to make itself ready for liberation. After all, I know that I do not behave impeccably. And surely I have read somewhere that enlightened beings are always impeccable. So I am ruled out of being a member of the enlightenment club.

This thinking traps me in duality. For now we have two things—oneness and non-impeccable behaviour which lies outside it.

We insist that oneness conforms to our rules to satisfy us that it is a proper oneness, a worthy oneness. Oneness, we think, cannot appear as cruelty or as dishonesty or as starvation in Africa. The mind says that there must be oneness with many things outside it, all the things we will not allow to be oneness. So the mind insists always that there are two.

The mind with its desire for justice will never be satisfied with just this.

This is why many spiritual teachings say that we must go beyond the mind. These teachings see the entrapment that the mind produces but they fail to see that there is no one who is entrapped.

There is no one who can go beyond the mind. When there is no person and no mind it is seen that entrapment is also liberation.

The self, with all its barnacles and peccadilloes, is also liberation arising as the self. When this is seen it is known that questions of honesty, correct behaviour, morality and justice are irrelevant. All these concepts lose their meaning when it is seen that there is no one making any choice. Courage and cowardice, honesty and dishonesty, truth and lies, justice and injustice, responsibility and irresponsibility are just a play of light, oneness appearing as everything that manifests.

But to the mind the suggestion that starvation in Africa and lies and injustice are also oneness is an abomination.

This book is not intended for those who want to satisfy the mind's desire for nobility and justice.

There is only liberation. Searching for liberation is also liberation. Otherwise there would be duality. There would be oneness and outside oneness the search for it.

The search for liberation is simply liberation pretending not to be itself and looking for itself. For this to work the pretence has to be very effective. Otherwise oneness would instantaneously find itself and the game would be over before it could begin. And the pretence is very effective for although everything is this, the mind sees everything as that.

Actually the mind often does think that it has glimpsed liberation, but it only ever thinks that it has seen it over there—perhaps in the person of that holy sandaled one with the brilliant aura and the peacock feathers, surrounded by their fascinated devotees.

Of course this is all metaphor. There is no game. There is nothing looking for something. Try reading that last sentence in both possible ways.

This is a dream but I am not having the dream. I am a dreamed character within the dream. This is why it is not me who wakes up.

Oneness already knows itself and has no need to find itself because it is not lost. But because liberation is not personal, the mind, which is personal, can never get it.

If you have a lively mind, as many seekers do, this bears repeating. The mind can never get this. Thinking I have understood this has nothing to do with liberation.

The seeker cannot help seeing liberation as magical and creating fantastical imaginings about it. We yearn for the gifts that we think liberation will bring. This may make us prey to every passing guru, spiritual teacher and mantra salesman.

But in liberation it is seen that liberation is entirely ordinary but also wonderful. This is a paradox. The seeing of liberation is simply everyday life, the squirrel on the tree trunk, with the veil of seeking taken away. The roller-coaster ride of the neurotic mind becomes a gentle wonderment.

But the mind may not like the loss of its neurosis.

Thoughts create the appearance of there being a person who has a mind. For the self-conscious seeker many of these thoughts may be about finding out who 'I' truly am. But the apparent person who seems to be having these thoughts does not exist and thought itself cannot discover its own nature. It has no nature to discover.

In liberation it is seen that thoughts arise from emptiness, from nothing and from nowhere. They simply arise and fall away. Thoughts do not go anywhere and they do not lead to anything. They have no significance.

Depending on the patterned nature of the body-mind, opinions, leanings, prejudices and beliefs may all still arise when liberation is seen.

But it is unlikely that they will be taken seriously.

Awakening is seeing the emptiness of the void.

Liberation is seeing the fullness of the void.

Contraction and Localisation

In the explosion that is the seeing of liberation contraction ends. This is not to say that the experience of a contracted person cannot return because anything is possible in liberation. But there is a strong tendency for contraction not to occur once liberation is seen.

However localisation, the sense of there being a body-mind in a particular place, is different to psychological and emotional contraction. For this body-mind, when liberation was seen, any sense of localisation ended for a while. Awareness was seen to be everywhere. The room in which standing was happening, the street in which there was walking, the bodies and lamp-posts and benches and space that were appearing, were not differentiated in their belonging from this arm, this thinking process, this seeing, these feet walking the pavement. There was no sense of anyone walking past anything or through any space. Yet it was noticed that the body was able to negotiate apparent space and time without colliding with either walls or the future.

Some time later the sense of localisation returned and it was felt once more that there was a body occupying a space-time dimension. But the sense of contraction that had been a constant part of this life, even after awakening, was gone.

With liberation comes the seeing that there is only unconditional love arising as everything that is. There can be no explanation for this although the mind will look for one. It simply is so.

When 'I' am seen as everything there can be no possibility in that seeing except to realise that everything is love.

Death and Religion

Question: How do you find out what happens after death?

Answer: You ask someone who has died.

Last night I dreamt that I was having dinner in a restaurant with an old friend. We asked for the bill but before it came I woke up. Did my friend have to pay my share of the bill?

It is easy to see that the question about my dream is absurd. It is the same with the question "What happens to me after death?" The question dissolves when it is seen that I am a dreamed character. Then it is seen that there is no 'me' who dies, no 'after' because time is created only in the dreamed mind and no 'death' because death is simply the awakening from the dream.

If there were anyone who could choose not to worry, I would say "Don't worry. It will be alright."

But the mind cannot imagine its own annihilation. Faced with the appearance of death in the dream, the mind creates stories about its own continued existence after death. All of these stories are like answers to the question "Who pays the restaurant bill of the dreamer who wakes up before the bill arrives?" We are all familiar with so many of these stories. Most offer some variation of reward for a life well-lived, however that is conceived, and punishment for a life of evil doing. They are both seductive and intimidating, alternately promising us spiritual riches and threatening us with dire torments.

In fact there are billions of these stories because each one is unique to the particular dreamed character who holds it. My version of salvation through the blood of the lamb will be different to yours. Your version of taking rebirth as a god, a human, an animal, a hungry ghost or a demon will be different to that of the Buddhist meditator sitting next to you.

In most of the stories that the mind spins around death there are a few common themes. There are rules to be obeyed. There is effort to be made. There are bad actions to be avoided and good ones to be carried out. There are rewards to be earned by following the instructions of the pastor, priest, lama, guru, yogi or swami. Buddha or Jesus or Krishna may be invoked to justify these rules. There are threats of future punishments, often of extreme torture, to encourage you to keep on the path. In some versions of these stories, for example the cruellest amongst the Christian ones, these punishments last for all eternity. In other slightly more compassionate versions, like some within Buddhism, they only last for an unimaginably long time. In some of these stories you do not have to murder a convent of nuns or go to a drug-crazed orgy to destroy your chances of a blissful after-life. For some people, simply dancing on a Sunday will do that.

The structure of some minds can even manifest the appearance of ghouls, ghosts, spectres and spirits. This helps to persuade the mind that it will continue after death.

For many seekers the most seductive of the stories about death is the story of karma and rebirth. This appeals particularly to the mind which likes justice, because this story makes everything seem just and so personal suffering appears more bearable.

The story of karma is the story that each of my actions and thoughts bears fruit exactly according to its nature. Clearly this is not the case in this lifetime for the 'evil' are often seen to prosper and the 'saintly' to suffer. So the story of karma usually includes the story of rebirth. Every apparent injustice is explained and swept away by this story from deformities at birth to the billions amassed by despots to the broken leg as someone unexpectedly trips and falls down the stairs. To the mind this story is extremely satisfying. If my abuser prospers in this life he will suffer in another when he is reborn as a toad. If my self-sacrificing goodness and asceticism goes unrewarded in this life at least I will attain a favourable rebirth. Perhaps I will have an enhanced golden aura which will attract followers to whom I can teach the attainment of enlightenment.

The idea of karma and rebirth develops from a person's belief in volitional action. Volitional action is the choice to do something, to exercise free will. When it is seen that there is no one, it is seen that there is no possibility of volitional action. There is no one who makes any choice of any kind. Cause and effect fall away when it is seen that all apparent actions simply arise without volition out of nothing.

However, if we want an explanation of personal suffering that will satisfy the mind, there is an enormous store house of religious beliefs that we can choose from. There are enough religions to suit everybody's tastes from the most ascetic to the most luxuriant. We can dress ourselves in hair shirts and whip ourselves with flails or put on scarlet robes and feast our eyes on golden statues. We can revere celibate men who instruct us on how we should conduct our sex lives or look forward to a paradise where we can watch gleefully as our enemies burn in hell.

There are even secular religions like Saving The Planet or Socialism. Or we can combine the secular and the spiritual and invent our own religion such as Transcendental Politics or Psychotherapeutic Buddhism or Tantric Green Environmentalism.

Any religion may be able to satisfy our desire for meaning and purpose and offer an explanation for personal suffering. None of this has anything to do with liberation.

What happens at death cannot be understood
until there is no one to understand it.

A Life Left in Ruins

In some ways liberation may be considered to be a great catastrophe which can leave your life in ruins. Everything previously considered important may be taken away, especially if the life previously led was the life of a spiritual seeker.

Spiritual seeking fulfils so many needs. From it I may get meaning, purpose, hope, help, friendship, support, and structure to my life as I work to pay for my next retreat. Even in a split-second of awakening all of this can disappear. For some people it is possible after awakening to continue going through the motions, to still attend the full moon meditations or the gatherings at the feet of the guru for the craic, the friendship and the sense of community. But this can be risky. If the other devotees sense that you are no longer taking the search seriously, no longer treating the guru or mantra or ritual or belief with a genuine sense of devotion, then you could be the next human sacrifice staked out in the sun. Or at least you may be ejected from the group or made to feel so uncomfortable that you feel forced to leave.

And yet liberation is what we yearn for. We want

to lose everything, to be emptied out, to fall into the void. This is what we hope for although we cannot imagine what it is. We long to disappear.

Liberation is wonderful but it is not wonderful for anyone. So there is no advantage to be gained by anyone in the disappearance of the self.

The disappearance of the person is a death. So much of what the mind considers to be irrevocably a part of the person falls away—hopes, memories, even the neuroses which we hate and yet which feel comfortably familiar. Relationship and meaning end and suddenly this life is seen to have no purpose. All my beliefs, all my self-importance, all my sense of going somewhere end in a moment. My hopes of personal happiness and self-improvement vanish.

This is both greatly feared and deeply longed for. Although I cannot imagine what life could be like when I am gone or even that there could be a life when I am gone, something knows that this is the only possible redemption and salvation. I have to die for the pain of separation to end.

This is why it is worth repeating the great blessing I was given. I hope you die soon.

Natural and Neurotic Feelings

Seeing liberation brings neither a permanent state of bliss nor an end to suffering—only the end of personal suffering.

Anything can arise in liberation but there is a tendency for neurotic feelings to lessen or die away while natural feelings continue to arise. Natural feelings include anger, sadness, fear and happiness. In liberation these simply arise and fall away again and are seen for what they are. They may even become more powerful as they are no longer attenuated by the self and its neurosis.

Neurotic feelings such as guilt, embarrassment, anxiety or irritability tend to disappear in liberation as they are no longer sustained by a belief in a person or in meaning or in the possibility of personal success or failure.

Hope and despair of course are gone.

Although anything can arise in liberation it is unlikely that boredom will. Boredom is an experience of the personal mind. In liberation everything becomes fascinating—the shape of a hand, the taste of coffee, the sound of car tyres on a wet road.

Boredom is presently unknown here.

After liberation, which is really the death of the person, what remains is still a functioning body-mind with a character and patterns of behaviour. There will still be preferences and interests, character traits, perhaps eccentricities and foibles. The character may still prefer to drive a Honda rather than a Ford, to holiday in France rather than in Scotland, to eat their eggs boiled rather than poached.

The idea of the spiritual being, perfectly poised in calm detachment with no likes or dislikes greeting everything with equanimity, is just another construct of the mind. It is a spiritual fairy tale woven out of the need to see enlightenment as special and different, as being far removed from what I am today.

It is fairly easy for a certain type of disciplined and ascetic character to cultivate a detachment which will be attractive to many seekers. This detached asceticism will attract those who feel that holiness and discomfort are nearer to divinity than devilment and silk sheets. But it has nothing to do with liberation.

After liberation the character may still be famously bad-tempered, or fabulously lazy, or may insist on being at the airport three hours too early to make sure they catch their plane.

Therapy and Meditation

Some people, while searching, will go to a therapist. It is quite possible that therapy will make the person happier, at least for a while.

R. D. Laing regarded therapy as a way for us to get out of our prison. He favoured therapies that help us to simply get up and walk out. The door of the prison is in any case always open, he said. He criticised therapies which encourage us to sit there and analyse why we are in the prison. He could not see the point of someone sitting in a prison with the door wide open but saying "I refuse to leave until I understand in detail exactly why I was put in here." He was referring here to therapies that involve a lengthy examination of the past, or rather of 'the past' as the client and the therapist together construct it.

Actually therapy will never get us out of the prison that we think we are in. The prison is our sense of separation and only liberation can reveal that there never was a prison in the first place. However, therapy may make the unreal prison more comfortable, perhaps considerably more comfortable. And for a person to spend their time making their prison more comfortable is a sensible thing to do.

However, therapy will happen or it will not. And it may be seen that there is no one who can do anything about this.

Meditation is another way of making the apparent prison more comfortable. Meditation can be delightfully relaxing and it may gradually reduce the person's neuroses. But it is not going anywhere and there is no one meditating. There is no one who is being purified or brought closer to enlightenment by it.

I have taught meditation for many years and I know that it can induce highly refined personal experiences. These are likely to be interpreted by the seeker as spiritual, as signs that purification is taking place and that enlightenment is coming nearer. If that is what is sought, that is what may be found.

Although such experiences are no more valuable than eating toast, they are certainly no less valuable. And it may be seen that there is no one who either meditates or eats toast.

Paradise is Now

Until we lose our life we spend the whole of it looking for paradise. Sometimes looking for paradise involves killing a lot of people by putting them to the sword, burning them at the stake or blowing them to bits. Sometimes looking for paradise involves spending a great deal of time on our knees, beating ourselves with flails and eating a lot of gruel. Sometimes looking for paradise involves ministering to the sick, adopting Rumanian orphans or beating our version of God into the heads of heathen peoples. Often looking for paradise involves working very hard at a job we don't very much like so that we can buy a Mercedes, a house by the sea or a Rolex watch. Much of this is noble, much of it ignoble. All of it is divine.

Often there is an expectation that paradise will not be found until death. The mind creates wonderful stories about what this will be like. It can generate versions of these stories endlessly. Some may include several virgins and some bowls of dates. Some may involve the playing of harps and the endless adoration of God. Often they involve beautiful landscapes. Some years ago I heard a radio programme in which a sweet old Tasmanian man talked about a near-death experience he had when he was fourteen. His story involved a lush green landscape by a river and meetings with dead relatives. He asked a stranger in a matter-of-fact way "If this is heaven, where's Jesus, then?" to be told "Oh, he's just over there, down by the river talking to some people."

But a near-death experience is not a death experience. And no one ever gives a first-hand account of one of those on the radio.

Always there is the expectation that paradise will not be found until the future. Rarely is it noticed that by definition the future never comes.

The mind cannot help searching for paradise. It is its function. The mind is a device for obscuring the fact that paradise is now by putting it off endlessly through the phenomenon of dissatisfaction. There is nothing wrong with the mind doing this. It is simply what it must do for as long as there is a person.

In liberation it is seen that this is already paradise. The ticking of a clock is paradise. The taste of a grape is paradise. The rustling of leaves is paradise. The warmth of the foamy washing-up water is paradise. The sensation of feet brushing against carpet is paradise. What the mind finds boring is seen as wonderful.

This is an ever-changing never-changing miracle.

THE AVATAR OF
THE SINGLE MALT

HE WAS SHORT, PLUMP AND CHARISMATIC with dark soft eyes. He wore smart Indian clothes and a shawl embroidered with gold thread. His name meant The Teacher Who Is The King Of Bliss. To his devotees he was not just a guru. He was the avatar of this age. He had been Krishna, Buddha and Jesus. At least four other teachers claimed to be the one and only avatar at this time but his devotees scoffed at them. They knew that theirs was the one.

Then the shit hit the fan.

The guru, it appeared, had seduced three different women, all high up in his organisation, by telling each of them "I am the reborn Jesus and you are the reborn Mary Magdelene. Two thousand years ago we were lovers. Now it is time for us to be lovers again." As a line for the seduction of the credulous it is hard to beat. Each woman in turn had believed him and followed him to his bed.

One day the three Mary Magdalenes discovered that each of them was not unique. The game was up. They felt seduced, traduced and scorned. Outraged, they decided to expose everything. A hasty meeting was urgently convened. Phones rang and devotees were summoned.

The three Marys had been covering up many others of the guru's peccadilloes, hiding them from his public, sweeping empty whiskey bottles under the mat. Now it was open season and all the bony skeletons tumbled out of the cupboard with a rattle that would have wakened even the dimmest of the chelas.

The guru had been indulging in prodigious bouts of drinking. He sometimes consumed a whole bottle of whiskey before going on stage to address his devotees. Another bottle might be downed later in the evening. The inner circle of devotees had been busy keeping him supplied, hiding the evidence, smuggling out the empty bottles from the retreat centre. On at least one occasion he had to be helped onto the stage and onto his red velvet throne by an acolyte on each side propping him up to hide his stagger.

Perhaps his remarkable ability to weave impromptu a coherent tapestry of spiritual ideas while pickled in scotch was evidence of his divine status. The avatar of the single malt. The alcoholic godhead.

The guru had occasionally given out spiritual names, but only to particularly special devotees. These names, he said, were arrived at in deepest meditation when he tuned in to the most refined spiritual essence of the person and emerged with the name whose vibration exactly suited their unique dharma. Then someone noticed that these were the names of the houses that the guru passed in an Indian quarter of Cape Town as he drove from his house to his office each day.

He had been enormously profligate with money, spending lavishly on himself.

There were even accusations that he had been seen beating his wife and her daughter.

Why had his acolytes kept all this to themselves? By the time they had realised what they had got themselves into, they were too far steeped in blood to draw back. They had given up careers, lovers, homes to follow this man. They had devoted oceans of energy to what they believed was the divine plan.

In this way the guru gave at least some of his devoted followers the gift of inoculation against gurus for ever.

There is a place for charismatic charlatans. They can remind us not to take this seriously. In the story more may be learned from a charlatan than from a saint.

An Edited Transcript of an Interview Recorded with Richard in July 2005

I'd like to start by asking you about something that you have written. You have said that language can only describe duality, so why attempt to talk about non-duality?

Well, there's only the possibility of using language or staying silent. There's no particular reason why we shouldn't stay silent, but sometimes it can be entertaining to talk. There's no possibility of describing non-duality in words because words are determinedly dualistic. Words separate things into this and that, here and there, now and then. However, words are all we have to communicate about this with. Perhaps they can point us towards non-duality and help to strip away misconceptions. Maybe they can describe what non-duality isn't and it's possible that out of this can arise something of interest.

Perhaps I should have started by asking the obvious question. What is non-duality?

Non-duality is simply a word that attempts to

describe the reality that there is only oneness aris-ing as everything and that there is no separation. Within the dream of duality things and people will always seem to be separate but this is simply an appearance. Non–duality sees through the appearance. Perhaps I should throw in even at this early stage that a person always lives irredeemably within duality, but that which sees duality is simply oneness. That which sees this is not the person.

This whole thing seems difficult to grasp.

No. It's impossible. It's impossible to grasp!

It may help our readers if you say something about what happened to you at Charing Cross Station. What was that about?

(Laughs) Ah yes, Charing Cross Station. It must be understood that it's very important that it was Platform 5.

Is that the platform that we all need to go to?

Yes. That's the platform with the plaque and the shrine and the eternal flame.

And vestal virgins?

Well, the railway staff attend to the shrine very

lovingly. I've asked for some vestal virgins but they say they haven't got the budget and they can't get the virgins *(laughs)*.

What happened there was very simple but it is very difficult to describe. And it is impossible to understand unless it's been seen. What happened was the complete and instantaneous disappearance of the person. I say 'what happened' but it wasn't really something that happened. It is so difficult to talk about this because in the appearance things happen in time. When the person disappears it is not an event that happens in time. It is seen that this happens outside time and that everything is timeless.

Within the story the person who has disappeared comes back very quickly. That's what happened here anyway, and my understanding from talking to other people and reading other people is that this is quite common. So there may be an instantaneous total disappearance of the person and then a split second later the person returns, quite probably in a state of shock and saying "What the hell was that about?" But although the person returns something irrevocable has happened. An irrevocable change has taken place in the apparent individual. And this may be different for each person, so really all I can do is talk about what it was like for this character. I can talk about what changes this character experienced after that if you like. Very little else can be said about the event itself. I have tried to describe it in my writing but it is very difficult. All I can really say is it's unimaginable. I can invite you to imagine it but it's impossible.

I invite you to imagine being here as you are and then suddenly for a split second everything remains absolutely the same as it is right now except that you are not in it. Yet there remains complete awareness of it. Sometimes this is called an awareness of the void or an awareness of emptiness because the self is seen to be completely empty. In a way I feel that's a fairly accurate description but the problem with describing this is that it cannot possibly be imagined. Where there has been a person constantly for thirty or forty or fifty years, this does not relate to any experience which that person has had at any time in their apparent life. When the mind hears a description of this disappearance it tries to relate it to some experience that the person has had. The mind will try to make sense of it by relating it to a personal experience. But it was not a personal experience because there was no person there. There is no possibility of understanding this event in relation to anything that has gone before.

It didn't happen to a person? It didn't happen to you? That's very difficult to grasp.

It's impossible. As long as there has always been a person there experiencing things it cannot be conceived. Well, it can be thought about but what it is like when the person is not there cannot be known.

There seems to be something problematic about trying to discuss this at all.

Absolutely. It's totally problematic.

Would it be helpful to compare that event with what happened in the clothing store?

We have to use language so let's say that what happened in that first event was awakening. What that means is a sudden seeing that there is no one, a sudden seeing of this, that this is all there is, totally unmediated by the self. And there was the realisation that everything that had been experienced before had been mediated through the self, the subjective self, if you like. On Charing Cross Station there was the sudden split second seeing of the complete absence of the self. This is sometimes described as the seeing that I am nothing. Nisargadatta has said that seeing I am nothing is wisdom. And as I have said this brings about, or for this being it brought about, irrevocable changes.

In the story of a person, which is completely meaningless, the second event happened about a year later. Actually it happened outside time and in eternity. It's very difficult to describe this. Within time, let's say, so it kind of makes sense as a story, there was a much longer event. Again, this was not an experience because there was no person there to have the experience. There was a much more gentle total disappearance of the person but this time what was seen was that awareness was 'everywhere'. As I use that word I know that it's misleading, because 'everywhere' implies space and part of this awareness is that there is no space. So awareness is everything and everywhere and every non-thing and nowhere. To tell a story about that is to try to summon up a picture which it's impossible to summon up.

I just happened to be in a clothing store at the time buying my son a suit, and what was seen was that awareness, or the sense of 'I' if you like, has nothing to do with the person whatsoever. What was seen was awareness arising as everything, so that awareness was equally 'in' the environment, the walls, the floor, the ceiling, the carpet, the street outside, the noises that passed, and the customers and assistants, but also 'in' the space in between these apparent things. That's what I mean by saying that awareness is everywhere. So awareness was equally here where the physical body seems to be and over there where the wall seems to be and in between the two. Because it was seen that there is no over here or over there or in between. The wall and the space is just as much awareness as the person or the customer.

In the story of a person this event lasted for a while and I can't possibly explain what I am going to say next. It's simply a mystery, but in this event it was also seen that everything is unconditional love. This is nothing simply arising as unconditional love. The wall and the person and the space between is unconditional love. And there's nothing further I can say, I feel, to correlate these two things. I can't even suggest that there is a causal connection. All I can do is to report that seeing "I am everything" also contained "Everything is unconditional love." And to go back to Nisargadatta, he said that seeing I am nothing is wisdom, seeing I am everything is love. And so that's what is described in my writing as liberation.

What that brought about, to use terms to do with time and the story, was the complete end of seeking; the end of the sense of separation which had led to searching for something to make it feel easier. And it was seen then and it has been seen since that this is it. There is nowhere to go, there is nothing to seek, everything is complete in this.

You have talked about the sense of separation—that everything is fuelled by the sense of separation. Can you say what is meant by that?

What is meant by that is the sense of a self which feels itself to be separate and therefore vulnerable and therefore threatened. All the apparent activity of the person is motivated at its core by the desire to end this sense of separation.

Now for most people most of the time this will not be realised consciously. So most people feel their sense of loss, their sense of vulnerability, their sense that this isn't it, as a sense that they would be fulfilled if they got a new car or promotion at work or if their lover was kinder to them or if they got a new lover or a bigger home in the country.

It is only sometimes realised as a more existential sense of loss. But nevertheless, everything that the individual seeks to do, all their motivation to get a kinder lover or a bigger home, is at its core fuelled by the feeling that this isn't it.

The feeling that there is always something missing and the fear of vulnerability and that somehow I can do something to heal that—that's what I mean by the sense of separation. Everything is fuelled by the sense of separation.

Let's refer to your comment about the past having become two dimensional. What do you mean by that?

I can try to suggest what I mean. I can try to describe it inadequately in words. This is something that I refer to when I write about the split second event of awakening. Although the person came back, as I have said in answer to a previous question irrevocable changes took place. One of those irrevocable changes was that the past had lost its substance. Before that event the extent to which this person had lived in the past was quite considerable, as it is for many people. In other words, nostalgia was quite a big impulse, regret was a reasonably big impulse in this person. With regret there sometimes went guilt. For example, as for many people, this mind would sometimes play over the past. I would ruminate on scenes from the past. I would regret that things had turned out as they did. I would wish they were different. The mind would turn over what this apparent person had done. The past was a very real place. Memories of it had considerable substance in the imagination.

What was noticed after this split second of awakening was simply that this had ended. All I can do is report on this. I can't even draw a causal connection. After awakening the person came back and in many ways was still an unhappy person but the reality of the past was seen through. It was no longer possible to reconstruct the past vividly and there was very little impulse to visit it anymore. I say in my writing that this is not Alzheimer's *(laughs)*. This is not loss of memory. It was still just as easy to remember, for example, an apparent event that might have happened on the first day of school but there was no impulse to remember such an event. And if for some reason the mind did flicker back to that it was without energy. The scene had no life to it anymore, there was nothing gripping about it, and so with the disappearance of the vivid imagery of the past regret and guilt also disappeared. There was nothing seen to be real about the past anymore, so there was nothing to feel regret or guilt about.

There is something attractive about that!

There is something wonderful about searching coming to a stop when liberation is seen.

So for this person in awakening everything ended, there was no one. There was no possibility of personal suffering, personal pain, anything like that. When the person came back the person's reaction to that was, "Wow! Bloody Hell!" But because the person was back the person's reality was also back. So the period after that, which lasted for a year, was quite a difficult one. There was still a variety of neurotic feelings. There was still boredom, irritation, a certain amount of despair. There was certainly still searching going on, very much a feeling of separation, and in a way I was worse off than before. Because although there was still a feeling of separation, now there was a knowing that none of the ways of seeking had any meaning to them. I had had three decades of seeking through spiritual means and psychotherapeutic means, and indeed I had built around myself a considerable raft of effective techniques with which to deal with uncomfortable feelings and uncomfortable thoughts. These worked very well for a while but they were always only temporary. They never actually healed the sense of separation. But they certainly made the prison more comfortable.

Now in a sense all these techniques fell away. This left despair without hope. This is why it is often said that the period between awakening and liberation can be experienced as a desert, a period of helplessness, hopelessness and meaninglessness. It is seen that nothing has any meaning, that nothing can be any help and there is no hope because there is no one who can do anything about their predicament. And yet the predicament still exists and so it can be quite a painful place.

It is sounding less attractive all the time.

(Laughs) Put very simply, in a couple of sentences instead of many paragraphs, what I am saying is that for this apparent character, after awakening when the person came back, searching very much continued. It was very, very strong. Then in liberation it simply stopped. There was no more searching. In a sense I could define the seeing of liberation as simply the end of searching but I wouldn't like to do that because it's so limiting. Once liberation is seen there is nothing needed, so what could there possibly be to search for? It's seen that there is no separation so the search has to end.

It makes an elusive kind of sense.

It's all elusive, I'm afraid

People reading this will struggle with it. It's deeply paradoxical and unexpected. Can you say more about what is meant by "There is no person"?

So in liberation it's seen that there is no person, and phenomena—feelings and thoughts, visual stimuli, tactile stimuli, aural stimuli—simply arise. That's what I mean by 'this'. There is the seeing of this, the seeing of whatever phenomena present themselves. In liberation it is seen that these phenomena simply arise in awareness without a person mediating them.

Clearly you and I are here having this dialogue. People will ask "How can you possibly deny that I am here in this room, that you are here?" Readers may even feel that you are having them on.

(Laughs) So this can't be seen until it is seen. What there is here *(gesturing towards himself)* is awareness and in that awareness everything arises. And part of what arises here, maybe, is a sense of a character. Whereas what is there *(gesturing towards the interviewer)*, I don't know, is perhaps the sense of a person? For many people these statements will be heard as provocative. For others they will be puzzling or intriguing. And for many people they will just be downright boring and they will move

away as rapidly as possible to something more interesting. But whatever the reaction of the person, whether it is to be provoked, intrigued, bored or fascinated, that will go on being there until it isn't. I mean that in two senses. It will go on until something else arises, which will probably be between three seconds and three minutes later, like making a cup of tea. But in the other sense the person may keep coming back to their reaction to that—you, for instance, may keep feeling provoked by these statements until that stops. And that will absolutely stop when the person disappears and then this will be undeniable. There will be no possibility of denying it.

And another thing—I know you have read my writing—another thing that you will find is that I assert very strongly that this has absolutely nothing to do with spiritual experiences. As someone who has meditated and practised many transpersonal techniques, there have been many spiritual experiences here. I was somebody who meditated and always associated that with progression towards liberation. Until that moment on Charing Cross Station. Then even when the person came back it was seen that there was no possibility that anything this character or person had ever done could possibly have anything to do with liberation. Whether a person has meditated for thirty years or been an alcoholic for thirty years is irrelevant because liberation has nothing to do with the person. If for you that is provocative, it will be until it isn't.

This sounds revolutionary in the area of spiritual matters.

It's not, though. This message, this communication if you like, has always been there. It's just not been heard very often because it is so much less fascinating than the story of spiritual evolution. The message that I am somehow a person who lacks something but who can do something to fill that lack, like sit cross-legged in a cave or burn joss sticks and chant, is so much more fascinating. That is the message that is mostly heard. But this message has always been there. It's just that there are not many people who are interested in it. Compared to tantric sex or trepanning yourself with an electric drill so you can see angels or gods, this sounds quite dull.

I don't know how long I've been speaking to you about this but I could speak a hundred times longer on spiritual matters if I could be bothered to. Unfortunately there is no one here any more who can be bothered to speak on spiritual matters.

Richard, can you tell us about your remark "I hope you die soon"? It's certainly not a traditional greeting!

(*Laughs*) One thing that I might make clear is that

this was a blessing conferred upon me. I'm merely passing it on.

For a period of time, before liberation was seen, I had been going to talks and dialogues with Tony Parsons and at the end of one of these I think that I was manifesting a certain amount of desperation *(laughs)*. I had been phoning Tony up reasonably regularly and he heard my despair down the phone. So at the end of one of these meetings I went up to him to have another word about my despair. He gave me a big hug and said "I hope you die soon." I feel this was a most wonderful blessing and I am passing it on.

For some apparent people, and clearly I was one of them *(laughs)*, a kind of desperation arises to have done with this, a fatigue with all the searching, a realisation that all the merits gained and techniques acquired will only ever bring temporary relief.

Maybe there was a getting in touch with what was fuelling the sense of seeking at its core, this sense of separation. And perhaps there was an understanding on some level that nothing else would end that sense of separation. The only redemption is the seeing of liberation. But really there is nothing that the person can do about this.

So Tony clearly picked up my despair and that was his gift to me, if you like. I won't say it was help because nothing helps *(laughs)*. What he meant was that he hoped that what would happen for me was the end of the personal self, the death of the personal self, which is the only possibility for seeing liberation.

What is sometimes said is that the self has to die for this to be seen. There is a problem with the language there because 'has to' implies some imperative or task. But all that's meant by that is this is already liberation, but it cannot be known, it cannot be seen, until the self disappears, until the self dies. If what you want is to see liberation then I hope you die soon too.

An Edited Transcript of a Talk Recorded in November 2005

The core of what we are talking about here is that there is no one, there is no person. The impression of there being a person is created as a kind of trick, an appearance. It seems that awareness has coagulated into this space where this individual, who appears separate from every other individual, is situated. What happens in awakening is that there's a sudden seeing, often only for a split second, that awareness is actually everywhere. This is seen by no one because in that split second the person isn't there anymore. While the person is present, the seeing of this is absent. Then suddenly the person isn't there and this is seen. Immediately after that the person comes back, possibly in a state of some shock.

When the person is back they may be inclined to spin some kind of fantastical story about this event and claim it as their own. Particularly if the person was following a spiritual path or hanging around with gurus before they disappeared, when they come back they may tell a story that involves their own spiritual development. They're likely to relate the event to some spiritual effort that they have made and think "That was something I achieved."

But in that split second it's seen that there is nobody who ever could have made an effort. The idea that an illusory person can get themself to see that they are unreal is completely absurd. I hope it sounds absurd. It's meant to.

This isn't the only way I've heard of awakening happening. There are people for whom there isn't this rather momentous split second event. They just seem to slide into this seeing almost without noticing it.

Later on there can be another event after which the person doesn't come back and the seeing that the person is simply an appearance remains. There can also just be a sliding into this. There doesn't have to be any kind of event which feels momentous. So now it's 'permanently' seen that there is no person. I'm using the word 'permanently' because the person doesn't come back to claim this event and it's now known that whatever appears to be happening has nothing to do with what was previously experienced as a person.

It's also seen that as there's no person, there's no choice. There's nobody sitting in this room who could make a choice. What's happening in this room is simply that awareness is listening to itself talking about itself because that seems to fascinate awareness some of the time.

Most of the time awareness seems to be more

fascinated with getting drunk in the high street or saving the planet or watching television. But some of the time awareness is fascinated by watching itself listening to itself talking about itself.

Leo Hartong uses the phrase *'awakening to the dream'* as the title of his book on non-duality. When liberation is seen, nothing changes in the world of phenomena. The car still has to be serviced, the cats still have to be fed, but now it's seen to be a dream. There's been a waking up but no one has woken up *from* the dream. There's been a waking up to the reality that this is a dream and the person is a character within the dream.

When you dream at night there's a certainty that what is being experienced is real. Perhaps you're running down a road after a horse which grows wings and flies off into the sky. While this is going on it's utterly convincing. A second later you wake up and then it's known that it was unreal. There's an absolute seeing when you wake up in the morning that the dream wasn't real, however convincing it felt when you were asleep.

Awakening and liberation are about waking to the dream that is ordinary life. While there's the sense of a separate person, there's an unarguable certainty that this is real. But when liberation is seen and it's clear that there is no separate person, this is seen to be a dream. Just as in the morning it's known that the winged horse wasn't real, it's now seen that the sense that there's a person sitting here who is separate from everyone else and who does things of their own free will isn't real.

I have dreams where I wake up with a real shock because they're so vivid.

However you wake up, whether it's with a shock or gently, there's still that certainty that what was known to be real while you were asleep is actually unreal. We could use lucid dreaming as a metaphor for liberation, because in lucid dreaming the nighttime dreamer knows that it's a dream.

Liberation doesn't change the phenomena that are experienced. If you follow spiritual paths and sit with gurus you tend to come across very exciting ideas about the phenomena of enlightenment. Enlightenment can sound like a wonderful state but liberation has nothing to do with this. In liberation, phenomena remain the same. It's simply seen that there's no separation.

So being awake and being asleep are the same, but that isn't how it feels if you're asleep. If you're asleep and become interested in this idea of waking up it seems as if there's something fascinating to be discovered. Spiritual paths tend to develop around this notion. The mind will spin complex stories about spiritual paths which play on the idea that there's something marvellous to be discovered and that there are wonderful people wandering about, probably in India, who have found it. One day I may discover it as well and then I'll have special powers and feel blissful all the time and my friends will envy me. This is just a story that the mind spins, but it's unlikely that I'll see that while I'm asleep.

There are many people communicating about non-duality. Lots of them call themselves 'teachers' and I'd be quite wary of these because there's nothing to teach about this. All we can do is try to give a description while acknowledging that non-duality is actually impossible to describe. As a description is impossible, we're bound to fail, so we can all relax now.

Spiritual teachers teach becoming, the need to improve a person who feels inadequate. A spiritual path is walked along by someone who feels they need to make themself into a better person so that they can deserve enlightenment. But the paradox is that as we set out on a spiritual path to make ourselves more adequate, there has never been anyone there who needs to be improved. And the idea of making choices becomes ridiculous and falls away when it's seen that there is no one. You are the divine puppet. You are a character that's breathed by oneness. How could you possibly be improved?

You could say that we are all perfect anyway, that we are all exactly how we should be.

Yes. But the character who is exactly as they should be does not feel themselves to be like that so they might go off to meditate or follow a spiritual path. Another very popular way to make yourself feel better is to do therapy. You can go through all that and in the end you may have a person who feels happier, but you still have *a person* so they will also still feel separate. There will still be a longing, a knowing that there's something missing. What's missing is the primal sense of unity that was there when we were born.

No matter what we do we will never heal the sense of separation because as long as there's a person there will be a problem. In fact the person is the problem. Therapy and meditation are both wonderful things to do and they'll probably make your prison more comfortable. But they don't get you out of your prison because *you are* the prison. The person can't possibly get out of their prison precisely because the prison consists of the sense that there is a separate person. This is what prevents us from recognising this as paradise. When the person drops away it's seen that there never was a prison and this has always been paradise. We never left paradise.

You can relax now because there's nothing which

can be done. You might as well give up. You are totally helpless. All choice is illusory. In the relaxation of that giving up it's possible that liberation might be seen.

I went through depression and I could see quite clearly that nothing was real and that nothing mattered.

It's all meaningless. It's Humphrey Bogart and Claude Rains on the cinema screen walking off into the jungle together at the end of *Casablanca*. When the film is over you can see it was just a play of light.

I knew nothing was real but other people felt they had to get me over that.

Well-meaning people come along and say "We've got to get you out of this because you're ill."

It was a bit frightening at times to know "I'm not here."

Yes. There's no one here. And thirty years ago, if you were talking about this, it's possible that somebody would be very concerned and suggest that you see a psychiatrist.

Yes, they did.

At that time, and it might still happen now, if it was expressed that "I am not a person", the interpretation could be that there's something wrong. Suzanne Segal writes about this in *Collision With The Infinite*. For her there was a profound disappearance of the person but she had no framework to fit it into. She was frightened and confused so for about ten years she went to see psychotherapists. They all felt there was something wrong with her that needed treatment because of the fear that she was expressing. It was only after this that she began to talk to people who knew about unity and liberation. Then the fear started to leave her and this began to feel OK.

In my case material things didn't matter after that experience.

It tends to produce a completely changed perspective when it's seen that nothing has any meaning. This isn't a depressing thing, it's simply seeing that all meaning is just a story of the personal mind. There's a thought-stream which creates the appearance of a person. Things often seem very meaningful to that person, whether it's religion or shopping or politics. And then that can all just be seen through.

So what might a psychiatrist say now to people who disappear?

It depends on the psychiatrist. If you're lucky you might find a psychiatrist who knows something about this. The best luck you can possibly have is to find a psychiatrist who isn't there *(laughs)*, a psychiatrist where there is no person. This would be rare. It depends partly on what is communicated about this when it's seen, because for some people it's a bigger shock than for others. There's a woman in America who spent two years just sitting around after seeing this. She wasn't in any sense unhappy but that seemed to be the only thing that could be done. After two years she began to communicate with people about it.

* * *

Are you saying that there's no free will?

I am saying that there's no person. So how can there be free will?

But I've got free will. I can walk home the usual way tonight or I can choose a different way. I feel I've got a choice.

Yes, of course you feel you've got a choice, because there's a person there.

So if there's no person, there's no free will?

There's the appearance there of a person who is making a choice. A thought comes up when you're walking home "I could go left here." Another thought comes up "I could go right here." A third thought comes up "I'm choosing left." It seems as if there's a choice. But these are just thoughts arising for nobody. The apparent choice as you go home and feel you can turn left or right has no reality whatever.

Interestingly there have even been scientific experiments recently that suggest that free will is an illusion. It has been shown that about a third of a second before a conscious intention to perform an action arises, the parts of the brain that are involved in that action activate. So about a third of a second before you have the thought "I shall turn left here", your brain is activating to turn left. Only after that do you have the conscious thought. This has staggering implications but it tends to be ignored because it conflicts with our paradigms about what it is to be a person.

We know there's intelligence but where does it come from?

Ultimately all you can say is it's a wonderful mystery. Thoughts arise from nothing. But the sense that there's a choice will very much be there as long as there's a person. Most of us will strongly resist the idea that there is no choice. We will often become angry at the suggestion because we feel that without choice so many things about being a person go out of the window.

One thing that goes out of the window is karma. The philosophy of karma depends on the idea that we make choices which then have an effect and that these effects always come back to us. This philosophy is usually tied up with the concept of rebirth because it doesn't seem to make sense without it. It's quite obvious to us that people don't necessarily get their just deserts. They can do terrible things and nevertheless flourish during their lifetime.

But the idea of karma depends on there being a person who has volition and makes choices. You even get this strongly in Buddhism. Many Buddhist teachings cling to the story of karma even though at its root Buddhism is very clear that there is no one, that the person is only an appearance. Karma is a wonderful story which the mind loves because it makes everything seem just. It's like an exactly accurate divine balance which weighs everything and hands out justice. It's also quite a juicy story because if people do hateful things, it's very satisfying to tell yourself that they'll come back as earthworms.

* * *

Most of the distress in my life has been about having very frightening thoughts. I couldn't bear to think anymore but I didn't know what to do about these thoughts. I wanted to stop thinking.

Who will stop thinking? Thinking arises or it does not. Usually it does arise, except in dreamless sleep, but there's nobody who is doing it. However in the story of spiritual paths, thoughts are often made an impediment. There's the idea that liberation is about going deeply into silence and for that to happen thinking has to stop. There then follows the idea that somehow the person can stop their thoughts. This is utterly absurd. What's seen in liberation is that there's nobody who is thinking, there's nobody who could stop thoughts. Thoughts aren't an impediment, they don't cover over silence. There is always only silence from which everything arises including thinking. The idea that there is a person who by an effort of will can stop their thoughts produces a great deal of strain and mental constipation.

I think it's more about allowing the thoughts that I enjoy to be there. I didn't want to think about bad things that upset me, so I kept these thoughts away by controlling them.

That's how it seems. But actually there's no one who's controlling them. There's nothing that can be done about thoughts just as there's nothing that can be done about anything. But at another time it might be seen that they're not a problem. Thoughts just flow.

With me now there's much more allowing of whatever thoughts there are just to be.

Even the understanding of this without the seeing of it might produce a profound relaxation. It might do but there's no necessity for that to happen. For some people it might produce intense frustration.

A lot of people don't want to hear this because it's going against what they believe even though you're not telling people "You've got to take this on." You're just telling them what you think.

To suggest that there is no person is the worst thing you could say to many of us. It's worse than suggesting that our religion is wrong because it's more fundamental to say that there is no person. Some of us get very upset by this. But mostly we're simply not interested. That's quite obvious if you go out on the street. Generally we're busy being interested in something else such as buying a new hat or saving the planet.

Sometimes I think "Why can't I be more like that?" They're more accepting of life.

That might be how it appears. That's what you feel but as long as there's a person, there's always something lacking.

I suppose I'm wanting something else.

Yes, there's always some kind of drive.

That's there. A drive. Yes.

There's always a driving dissatisfaction with whatever is the case and that dissatisfaction will usually be experienced as something like "I'm dissatisfied with my car or my job or my partner" or "I can only be happy when I get a bigger house." What's at the core of this dissatisfaction of course has nothing to do with my job or my partner or my car or the bigger house. What's at the heart of it is the sense of separation.

So if I have an awakening surely that means I could lose all my drive. People could lose all their drive to achieve things and that could be quite dangerous

(Laughs) Well, it's fortunate that there's no one who can do anything about it.

I might give up trying to achieve anything.

That could happen. You could become lazy. So what?

I've been through depression for a few years and I've definitely also had that sense that nothing matters. It was quite comforting. It felt like nothing was going to affect me, it was just happening. But this could lead to giving up, to laziness.

It depends on the character. This seeing that nothing matters could lead to laziness. So what? But if there's a character there who quite likes living in a house and the mortgage has to be paid for that to happen, then it's likely that the mortgage will still be paid.

But if people don't have that as their main focus they may just give up.

We're talking as if there's somebody doing this and there's a choice about it. But if you remove the idea of choice you just have a description. There can be liberation and absolutely nothing changes. Being awake and being asleep are the same thing. There are no whirligig phenomena.

There may be people who take this really literally so that if they have that occurrence of liberation, they'll just let everything go.

But there's no one who can choose to do that. That might happen or it might not but there's no one who can make that choice. Life just goes on.

The appearance just goes on. If you want exciting phenomena, take LSD. There's nothing you can do about liberation anyway but it's really uninteresting compared to taking hallucinogenic drugs. On an acid trip everything changes. In liberation nothing changes. It's just seen that there's no one doing it. So the mortgage will be paid or it won't be paid. But that's actually what's happening now anyway. There's no choice about it but you think you're doing it.

But if this actually happened, if I had an awakening and this actually happened to me—

Remember it doesn't happen to you.

OK. There may be an awakening and it's going to be quite a shock initially when the person gets back—

It may be.

So the person could be left thinking it's quite a negative thing.

They could be. The woman in America that I mentioned sat around for two years doing very little. What I'm trying to say is there's no choice about that. It will just be what it is. But actually that's what's happening already. At the moment you think you're doing something to pay your mortgage but you aren't. Work happens, salaries appear in the bank, mortgages get paid. There's nobody doing that. It's just that in liberation this is seen to be the case, whereas before that there's the idea that there's a person here who is doing something and if you get lazy then the mortgage won't be paid. But you cannot get lazy. However, laziness could happen. And it's possible that the mortgage might not be paid. But I suggest that if there's a character there who quite likes their comfort, just as there's a character here who quite likes his comfort (*laughs*), the mortgage will probably get paid. The mortgage here tends to get paid because this character would rather live in a house than live in a ditch, particularly in England. I suspect it would be the same for you. So I wouldn't worry about it. Not that there's anyone who can do anything about it.

But there are thoughts about what's worth striving for and I'm wondering, if there's awakening, would that all completely go by-the-by?

It's possible.

You still had a need to write your book.

Books get written.

Ah, books get written, yes.

People can get outraged by this. They say "If nothing matters that means I can go out and rob a bank!" This is a complete misunderstanding. There's no one who can choose to go out and rob a bank. Robbing a bank might happen but it's most unlikely to unless the person has the character of a bank robber. Robbing banks happens or it doesn't happen. Looking around this room, we are probably the sort of crowd where it won't happen. Although *(pointing to someone)* I'm not so sure in your case *(laughs)*.

So people who have had awakenings, are they saying that they are happier for it?

Not necessarily. A Zen monk once said "Now that liberation is seen, I am just as miserable as ever."

So we can't even pin that down, can we?

No, we can't even pin that down. But I would suggest that in the seeing of this, in liberation, there tends to be a kind of relaxation, a dropping away of certain things. One of the things that tends to drop away is neurosis. There's no necessity for this to happen of course. Anything can arise in liberation, including neurosis. Otherwise it wouldn't be liberation, it would be restriction. However, there seems to be a tendency for neurosis to drop away. So you may end up with an apparent person who is less neurotic and more contented. It also seems to me that boredom tends to drop away because in liberation, when there's no person in the way, everything becomes fascinating. How could you possibly be bored with the wonder of this?

So boredom and neurosis may drop away, but they don't have to. One way of putting this is that feelings like anger, sadness, fear and joy just arise naturally but neurotic feelings belong more to a person who is having personal experiences. When that person isn't there anymore these neurotic feelings and behaviours tend to drop away while natural feelings still arise. They might even arise more strongly because there's no person trying not to feel them and suppressing them. After liberation, anger for example might be experienced more profoundly than it was before, because before liberation there might have been a person there who was pushing their anger down.

Hence depression?

Hence depression.

★ ★ ★

Why do we need to sleep? It seems such a waste of time but I really enjoy it.

Oh, it's lovely.

Yes, I love it.

I do as well.

But it doesn't seem to be much use.

Oh it is you know. We would go mad without it. We have to sleep. We go home when we go to sleep. We are disassembled as a person. If you had to be a person for twenty-four hours a day you would go mad within a week. One of the fastest ways to produce psychosis is sleep deprivation. That will do it in about five days. It's used as a form of torture. We have to be disassembled. We can't bear to be a person for twenty-four hours a day. We need to spend at least eight hours in twenty-four not being a person.

It's still bizarre.

It is bizarre. The whole thing is totally bizarre.

★ ★ ★

We are like characters in a play. We have no choice.

We have no choice. 'Characters in a play' is a very good metaphor.

I am playing a character and so is everybody else.

114

It's not you that's doing it. It's oneness. There's a character arising in oneness. But there's a little trick going on which makes it seem that there is a separate person, that there is an individual in here and everything else is out there. In awakening, oneness recognises itself: "Oh. There is this dreamed character." Richard is just a dreamed character so Richard never wakes up.

Perhaps the characters in this room are getting little hints of their real nature.

Perhaps.

If what you are saying is true then maybe oneness has brought this character and everyone else to this place to get a hint of its nature.

Maybe.

Is that true?

What I'm trying to do here has got nothing to do with truth. It's simply to give a description. That's all. Truth is a very tricky concept. There are many versions of truth. Whose version would we be talking about?

If you're saying that oneness has brought you here to learn something about your true nature, you need to be a bit careful because you're starting to spin a story with meaning. "Life brought me here to this place so that something should be realised and that's very important." It's meaningless. It's just the same as when you wake up from your dream after sleeping at night. You can see that the night-time dream that was so real and so important when you were in it is completely meaningless.

This all seems very paradoxical.

Everything about this is paradoxical.

If I am a character in a dream...

Well, you are not. What you are is awareness. We could say that you're so much less than you think you are but also so much more. You're so much less than a person but you're so much more than that as well because you are awareness itself. You are the light in which all of this is happening. But that can't be seen until it's seen. What stops it being seen is the sense of the separate person because that seems so real. Until it drops away.

I think awareness as the light on the screen is a good metaphor. The characters aren't really there, are they?

No, yet they look so real.

They certainly look as if they're really there.

When you're in a darkened cinema you have to believe in these characters on the screen and yet it's just a play of light. There's nothing there. It's a very good metaphor. Perhaps we could say that liberation is like the lights in the auditorium coming on.

References

P. 18 "You can't stay in God's world for very long. There are no restaurants or toilets there."

Mariana Caplan, 'Halfway up the Mountain' Kindred Spirit Magazine (Summer 2000)

P. 28 "At death there is only liberation. It is just more chic to see liberation when you are alive."

Max Furlaud in a private conversation

P. 35 "Advaita is not an idea. *It is!* The lightning flashes, the eye blinks... Then? You have either understood or you have not understood... If you have not understood, too bad!"

Abhishiktananda

P. 45 "I'd love to give you something helpful, but in Zen we don't have anything."

Ikkyu quoted by Timothy Freke in 'The Wisdom of the Zen Masters', Journey Editions

Contact Richard Sylvester

Richard Sylvester lives in England on the border
of West Kent and East Sussex.

Richard can be contacted by e-mailing
richardsylvester@hotmail.co.uk

TO FIND OUT MORE VISIT
www.richardsylvester.com

Lightning Source UK Ltd.
Milton Keynes UK
UKOW051058130213

206231UK00001B/90/A